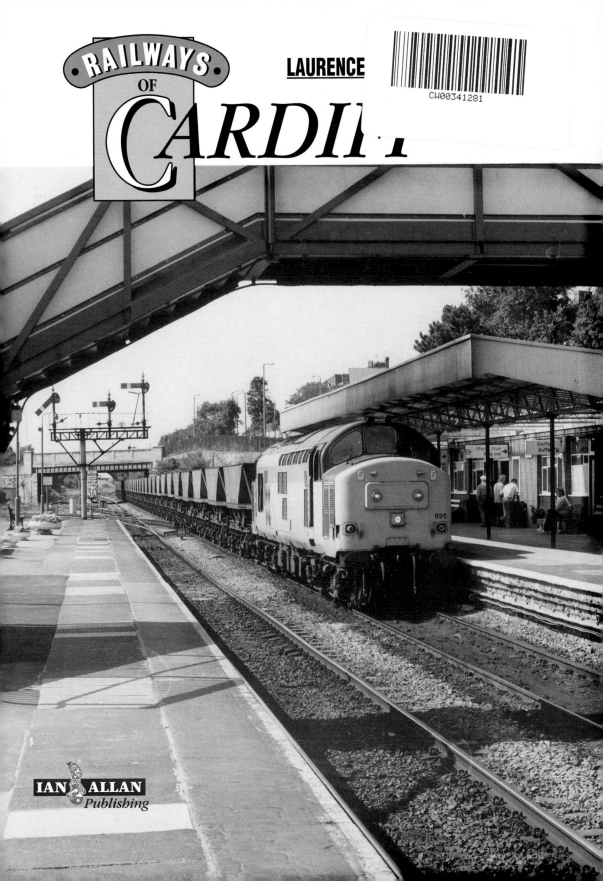

RAILWAYS OF CARDIFF

LAURENCE

IAN ALLAN
Publishing

First published 1995

ISBN 0 7110 2380 8

Published by Ian Allan Publishing

an imprint of Ian Allan Ltd, Terminal House, Station Approach, Shepperton, Surrey TW17 8AS. Printed by Ian Allan Printing Ltd, Coombelands House, Addlestone, Surrey KT15 1HY.

Front cover, top: A pair of Mirrlees engined Class 37/9s Nos 37905 and 37904 speed through Cardiff Central on 27 September 1994 with a down freight. A. E. Doyle

Front cover, bottom: 'Castle' class No 5048 Earl of Devon with the last down 'South Wales Pullman'. Hugh Ballantyne

Back cover, top: Cardiff Canton shed, November 1961. Hugh Ballantyne

Back cover, bottom: HST (No 43028) accelerates away from Cardiff on 27 September 1994 with the 12.57 'Shuttle' service from Paddington to Swansea. A. E. Doyle

It is impossible within the confines of a single book to adequately describe the rather complex history of the railways of Cardiff. There are many excellent books available that document, in much greater detail, the histories of the companies and lines mentioned within these pages. I hope, however, that what I have included is enough to whet the appetite of the reader to seek out more of the history of this most fascinating of rail centres.

Acknowledgements

Unless individually credited, all photographs and diagrams used in this book are from the Great Western Trust Collection at Didcot Railway Centre. I would also like to thank the following individuals and associations for supplying photographs and other material for this book: Chris Potts, D. Trevor Rowe, John Edwards, Paul Shannon, R. O. Tuck, S. Rickard, The Late Eric Mountford, The Great Western Trust and the Ian Allan Library. Special thanks to the following British Rail staff for their help with current and past operations at Cardiff: A. Carney (Station Manager Cardiff), Harold Williams (Duty Station Manager Cardiff), Mike Bates (Depot Manager Transrail Canton), David Roffey (Production Engineer, Transrail Canton), David Hallett (Operations Manager Regional Railways Canton Depot), Maurice Chelmis (Regional Railways Canton) and the staff of the Valley Lines control centre at Cardiff Central. Also to Ken Davies, Dane Garrod and Glenys Davies for reading and offering suggestions on the manuscript.

Contents

Introduction

During the 19th century many towns in the UK saw their prosperity grow with the arrival of the railway. This growth at Cardiff was probably not matched anywhere else. The phenomenal coal deposits of the valleys — at one time 72 pits were supplying 60,000 tons of coal each day — and the extensive iron and steel industry, together with Cardiff's great prominence as a natural port, saw what was a small provincial town grow within half a century into one of the largest and busiest shipping ports in the country. Some idea of this growth can be gleaned from the population which rose from 10,077 in 1841 to just over 183,000 by the turn of the century. Much of the industrial growth can be attributed to the second Marquis of Bute (1793–1848), the founder of modern Cardiff. For it was he, and after his death on 18 March 1848, his trustees, who constructed and ran the docks.

From 1 January 1887 the newly formed Bute Docks Company took over the running of the docks from the Trustees. The Bute West Dock had opened on 9 October 1839, Bute East Dock was partially opened on 20 July 1855, being fully opened on 14 August 1859. The Tidal Harbour was opened on 13 August 1856, Roath Basin on 23 July 1874, Roath Dock on 24 August 1887 and Queen Alexandra Dock on 13 July 1907. Returns for Bute West alone show that in 1840, 43,651 tons of coal and coke were exported from the dock, but by 1906 this figure had risen to a staggering 22,118,433 tons. Two other important docks were opened to the south of Cardiff. The first at Penarth was opened by the Penarth Harbour Dock & Railway Co on 10 June 1865, the second was opened at Barry by the Barry Railway on 18 July 1889. Although nominally not in the city both were very busy and generated much traffic locally.

The growth of the port at Cardiff also benefited other spheres of commercial activity with many other industries making Cardiff their home. The importance of the town was acknowledged when on 28 October 1905 it was constituted as a City.

Prior to the Grouping in 1923 Cardiff was served by no less than six different railway companies: The Taff Vale, the Rhymney, the Barry Railway, the Great Western, the Cardiff Railway and, via running powers, the London & North Western. The first three were so successful that prior to the turn of the century they were regularly paying dividends of $17^1/2\%$, 11% and 10% respectively.

Opposite:
Map showing the pre-Grouping lines at Cardiff.
Courtesy Railway Magazine

Following page:
Pre-Grouping passenger services at Cardiff.
Courtesy Railway Magazine.

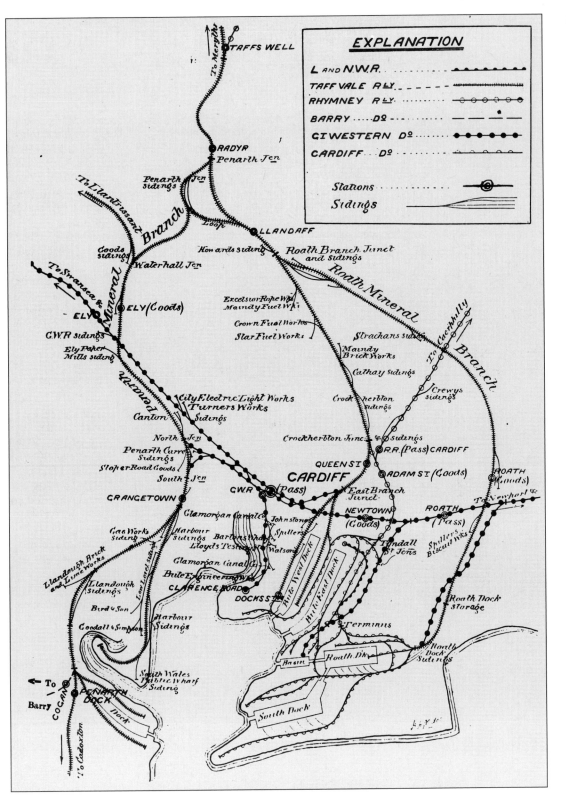

EXPLANATION

L AND N.W.R.	
TAFF VALE R⸺Y	
RHYMNEY R⸺Y	
BARRY .... D⸺o	
G⸺t WESTERN D⸺o	
CARDIFF ... D⸺o	

Stations

Sidings

TAFFS WELL

To Merthyr

RADYR
Penarth Jc⸺n

To Llantrisant

Penarth
Sidings

Branch

Loop

LLANDAFF

Howards siding

Roath Branch Junct
and sidings

Goods
sidings

Mineral

Waterhall Jc⸺n

Roath Mineral

To Swansea &c

Excelsior Rope Wks
Maindy Fuel Wks

Strachans sidg

ELY

ELY (Goods)

Crown Fuel Works

Star Fuel Works

To Caerphilly

Branch

G.W.R. sidings

Ely Paper
Mills siding

Maindy
Brick Works

Cathay sidings

Crews
sidings

City Electric Light Works

Crockherbton
sidings

Turners Works

Canton

Sidings

Crockherbton Junc⸺t & sidings

North Jc⸺n

Penarth Curve
Sidings

R.R. (Pass) CARDIFF

Sloper Road Goods

QUEEN ST

ROATH
Goods

South Jc⸺n

GRANGETOWN

CARDIFF
(Pass)

G.W.R.

ADAM ST (Goods)

East Branch
Junct

Glamorgan Canal

Johnstone

NEWTOWN
(Goods)

ROATH
(Pass)

To Newport &c

Gas Works
siding

Harbour
Sidings

Bartons Whf
Lloyds Testhos

Spillers
Watsons

Tindall
St Jons

Spillers
Biscuit Wks

Glamorgan Canal

Bute Engineering Wks

Bute West Dock

Llandough Brick
and Lime Works

Llandough
Sidings

CLARENCE ROAD

DOCKS ST.

Bute East Dock

Roath Dock
Storage

Bird & Son

Harbour
Sidings

Terminus

Goodall & Simpson

Roath
Dock
Sidings

To
Barry

COGAN

PENARTH
DOCK

South Wales
Public Wharf
Siding

Low Level Railway

Basin

Roath Dk

Dock

To Cadoxton

South Dock

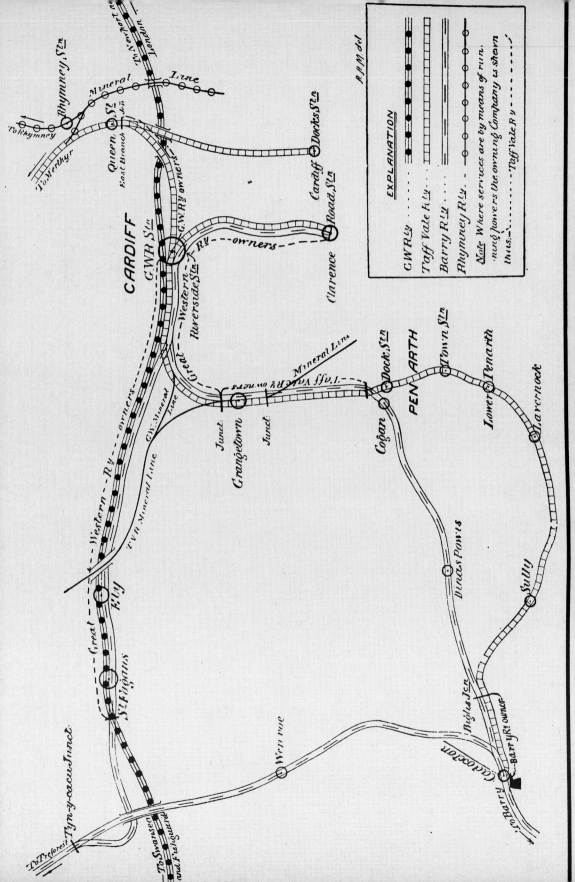

MAP SHOWING PASSENGER TRAIN SERVICES AT CARDIFF.

CHAPTER 1

The Growth of the Railway at Cardiff

T he first railway company to reach the Cardiff area was not, as might be supposed, the Great Western but the Taff Vale Railway. Operating the densest coal traffic in the world at the time over 124^1/$_2$ route miles, this company was the largest and certainly the most profitable of the independent companies operating into Cardiff. Prior to the opening of the line goods were shipped between Cardiff and Merthyr via the Glamorganshire Canal. The canal was opened in February 1794, but as with many other canals in this country a shortage of water in the summer coupled with the problems of freezing in the winter saw the canal out of use for long periods of time. It also did not help that over its 24^1/$_2$ miles the canal rose to a height of 543ft via 49 locks and barges were taking an average of three days to complete the journey.

It was against these problems that the Taff Vale Railway was formed. The company was incorporated on 21 June 1836 to construct a railway from Merthyr Tydfil down to the docks at Cardiff. It is interesting to note that although coal eventually became the most important commodity for the railway (by 1856 it was transporting 2^1/$_4$ million tons per year) the Company was initially formed to transport iron ore from the docks at Cardiff up to the ironworks at Merthyr. The line, which was engineered by Brunel using a gauge of 4ft 8^1/$_2$in, opened between Cardiff and Navigation House (Abercynon) on 8 October 1840, services being extended through to Merthyr on 12 April 1841. The line was opened as a single-track route and was not doubled until 1857. The use by Brunel of the standard rather than the broad gauge can most likely be attributed to cost together with the undulating nature of the line which was primarily designed for mineral traffic. At Cardiff the line terminated at Bute West Dock. Passenger traffic was also catered for with the construction of a small station in the commercial district of Cardiff, situated on the site of the current Queen Street station.

Previous page:
A view of West Dock taken in the mid-1880s. The photo was taken looking north from the footbridge of the Taff Vale's Cardiff Docks station, and also in view is the turntable of the nearby docks engine shed.

Below:
A view of old Cardiff shows tramcar No 45 passing through Queen Street around the turn of the century.

The Great Western arrived at Cardiff in 1850 under the guise of the South Wales Railway. Although initially an independent company the South Wales Railway was worked from the start by the GWR and was eventually absorbed by that company on 1 January 1862. The SWR was incorporated in August 1845 to construct a 143-mile broad gauge line from Chepstow to Fishguard via Cardiff, Swansea and Carmarthen, with the intention of opening up a new trading link to Ireland.

Unfortunately, troubles in Ireland coupled with a shortage of funds meant that construction of the final section to Fishguard was shelved. The line, which was also engineered by Brunel, was eventually opened in stages; the first section was opened between Chepstow and Landore on 18 June 1850, from Landore to Carmarthen on 11 October 1852, to Haverfordwest on 2 January 1854 and to New Milford (Neyland) on 15 April 1856. Interestingly, because the South Wales Railway was isolated from the main system, prior to the opening in 1850, locomotives and rolling stock had to be shipped across the Severn from Bristol.

Right:
Poster advertising the auction of Rhymney Railway locomotive No 7. The poster is slightly curious as records show that No 7 was a 2-4-0 tender engine built by the Vulcan Foundry in 1857 and again according to the records rebuilt as a saddle tank by the Rhymney Railway in 1881.

Below:
A very early view of Taff Vale Railway 0-6-0 Newbridge alongside the West Dock at Cardiff in 1849. The engine was constructed by Hick & Co, Bolton, in 1846.

E. R. Baker

CARDIFF.
TO BE SOLD BY
AUCTION,
(Under a Distress for Poor Rate), at the
RHYMNEY RAILWAY CO'S. FITTING SHEDS
ON THE EAST SIDE OF THE
EAST BUTE DOCK, CARDIFF,
AT ELEVEN OR TWELVE O'CLOCK,
On Tuesday, the 1st day of January, 1867,
A LOCOMOTIVE PASSENGER
ENGINE
of the best construction, built in the year 1858, No. 7.

D. DUNCAN, "CARDIFF TIMES" STEAM PRINTING OFFICES.

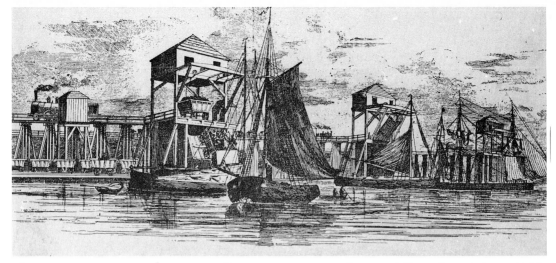

A small station was opened at Cardiff on the 18 June 1850 and stood on the site of the present Central station. It is worth noting that there was no direct connection between the SWR and the Taff Vale at Cardiff until 17 January 1854 when the SWR brought into use a short mixed-gauge line from its Cardiff station to connect with the Taff Vale at Bute Street Junction.

Through SWR services from South Wales to London were not introduced until the opening, via Brunel's Wye Bridge, of the one-mile connection between Chepstow and the Great Western's Chepstow–Grange Court–Gloucester line at Chepstow East on 19 July 1852. At Cardiff the SWR opened its own mile-long connection into the docks on 19 April 1858. During the weekend of 11-12 May 1872 the entire South Wales Railway was converted to standard gauge. The Great Western saw traffic to and from Cardiff, and South Wales in general, as an important part of its business and in 1886 the rather circuitous 170-mile route to London, via Gloucester, was cut to 153 miles with the opening of the Severn Tunnel to passengers on 1 December. In 1903 the distance was reduced even further to just 145 miles with the completion of the 'cut off' route via Badminton.

Although the Rhymney Railway (51 route miles) was incorporated on 29 July 1854 it was not until September 1857 that it entered Cardiff. The Act provided for the construction of a $9^1/_2$-mile line to connect the town of Rhymney with the Newport, Abergavenny & Hereford Railway at Hengoed. On 2 July 1855 the Act was amended to include a $9^1/_4$-mile extension from Hengoed to connect with the Taff Vale line at Walnut Tree Bridge. From here the Rhymney entered Cardiff via running powers over Taff Vale lines from Walnut Tree Junction, and via Crockherbtown Junction down to the coal tips at Bute East Dock. The first section to be opened was the dock branch in September 1857 but general goods services over the whole route were not introduced until 25 February 1858 with passenger services between Rhymney and its station at Cardiff Adam Street commencing on 31 March of the same year. The intense competition between the Taff Vale and the Rhymney saw the earlier co-operation considerably strained so it was no surprise when the Rhymney decided to open its own direct line from Caerphilly to Cardiff. At Cardiff the new line joined the Bute East Dock branch, the Cardiff Direct line as it was known being opened on 1 April 1871. From this date the station at Adam Street was closed to passenger traffic with trains using the new station at Cardiff 'Rhymney' (later Parade).

At this point one must also mention the London & North Western Railway which entered Cardiff via running powers over Rhymney Railway metals. The LNWR had extended its line from Brynmawr to Nantybwch during March 1864. At this time the Rhymney Railway was looking to extend its own line northwards from Rhymney to connect with the LNWR at Nantybwch and under a joint agreement the two companies agreed to build a joint line from Rhymney Bridge to Nantybwch. This three-mile line was opened for goods on 5 September 1871 (to passengers on 2 October that year). This, together with the opening of the southern section of the Rhymney between Caerphilly and Cardiff, gave the LNWR direct access to the docks at Cardiff and on 1 October 1875 the LNWR opened its own goods depot in the docks at Tyndall Street. Interestingly the LNWR line which served the three-storey warehouse was just 45 chains in length. Under a traffic pooling arrangement with the Great Western the former LNWR services into Tyndall Street were taken over by the GWR from 1 July 1933.

continued on page 15

Right:
Taff Vale Railway timetable dated 25 February 1859. Of particular interest is the term 'To-and-Fro' to denote return tickets.
British Rail

Opposite above :
Bute Street in about 1911. The large building on the right is the former Taff Vale locomotive depot. The depot was closed in 1857 and at the time of this picture was in use as a carriage shed.

Opposite below :
This wonderful poster by the artist Albert J. Martin was published in 1948 by the Docks and Inland Waterways Executive to promote the docks at Cardiff.

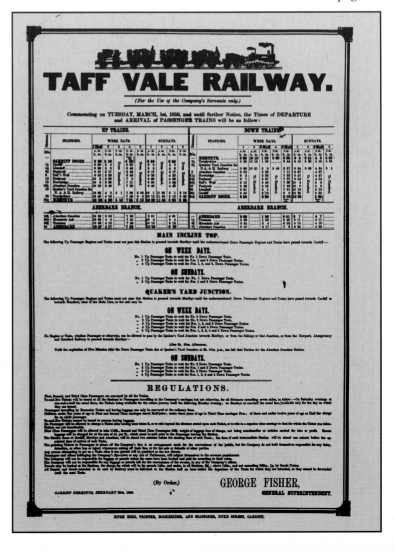

SOUTH WALES DOCKS
FOR QUICK DESPATCH

The Barry Railway Company (67³/₄ route miles) was established on 14 August 1884 to construct a branch connecting its new dock at Barry (opened on 18 July 1889) with the Aberdare coalfields.

The line ran from Cadoxton to connect with the Taff Vale at Tonteg Junction. It also connected with the Great Western main line at St Fagans via a short section from Tynycaeau Junction. The importance of the line and the dock can be gleaned from the fact that over a period of 10 years the annual tonnage of coal shipped from Barry exceeded 10 million tons per annum on no less than six occasions.

The Barry Railway direct route from Cardiff to Barry via Cogan actually evolved over a number of years. In August 1859 the Taff Vale Railway (under the auspices of the Penarth Railway) opened a six-mile branch from Radyr to the Tidal Harbour at Penarth. The new line also connected with the new dock at Penarth which was opened during 1865. The section from Cadoxton (originally called Biglis Junction) to Cogan, where it connected with the Taff Vale route from Cardiff, was opened by the Barry Railway on 20 December 1888. The first section of the now-closed coastal loop from Penarth to Cadoxton, the mile-long Penarth Extension Railway from Cogan Junction to Penarth Town, was opened on 20 February 1878. The remaining section was opened by the Taff Vale as far as Lavernock on 1 December 1887 but because of disputes over running rights the final section between Lavernock and Cadoxton was not opened until 22 May 1890. The branch from Barry Town to Barry Island was opened on 3 August 1896, services being extended through to Barry Pier on 27 August 1899.

Above opposite:
Some idea of the amount of coal traffic to the docks can be seen in this shot of the coal marshalling sidings at Roath Dock in March 1927. This was just one of many such yards.

Below opposite:
Cardiff Railway 0-6-2T No 28, renumbered 159 by the GWR, is pictured with a cattle train at Cardiff Docks about 1924.

Right:
Map showing railways in Cardiff c1958.
Ian Allan Library

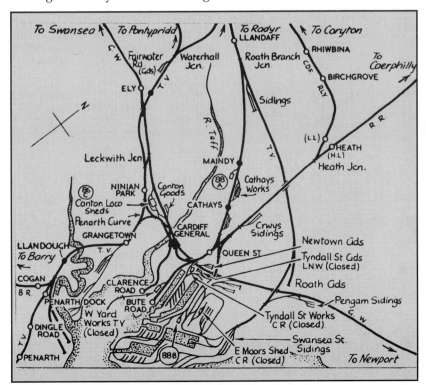

Above:
One of a series promoting the network, this 1952 poster puts the relationship of Cardiff and its railways into context.

During 1888 the Taff Vale Railway opened yet another connection into the docks at Cardiff. The Roath Mineral Branch was opened on 23 April. This five-mile line left the Taff Vale main line at Roath Branch Junction (Llandaff) and ran around the eastern side of the city to connect with the new docks at Roath and Roath Basin which had been opened in 1887. The increasing amount of mineral and general merchandise traffic being transported to and from the new docks saw the Great Western construct its own new docks line. The GWR's Roath Docks Branch was opened 2 November 1903. It left the GWR main line east of Cardiff at Pengam Junction and for about a mile or so actually ran alongside the Taff Vale's Roath Goods Branch into the East Dock area.

Railway development in the Cardiff area was completed with the formation of the Cardiff Railway. The company which was incorporated in 1897 initially took over the operations of the Bute Docks Company and the Marquis of Bute's Railway.

The Cardiff Railway was extended in 1909 with the opening of an 11-mile branch from Heath Junction to Rhydyfelin. Goods services were introduced between Heath Junction and Treforest on 15 May 1909 and passenger services between Rhydyfelin and Heath Halt on 1 March 1911. The northern section of railway was never very successful and on 20 July 1931 the branch was closed beyond Coryton. Interestingly a section of the branch, from Coryton to Nantgarw Colliery, was temporarily re-opened during August 1951 and until a new line connecting the colliery to the ex-TVR line at Taff's Well was completed in June 1952. Today the remaining section, from Heath Junction to Coryton, is part of the valley line service.

CHAPTER 2

Passenger Services

Services to and from Cardiff over the years can be divided into three sections: main line services to and from West Wales and London; cross country services to Birmingham, the north west, Bristol and the south and lastly the valley line services. Although the South Wales Railway opened its line through Cardiff in 1850 it was not until July 1852 that through services to London via Gloucester were inaugurated. Journey times averaged about 5hr but with the opening of the Severn Tunnel to passenger traffic on 1 December 1886 times were reduced (although in July 1887 just two services a day from South Wales to London were using the tunnel route). In 1888 the shortest journey time between Cardiff and London was 4hr 17min, but in July 1890 a new Severn Tunnel express service was introduced between Cardiff and London which cut the time to 3hr 53min. In May 1896 first class restaurant cars were introduced on some services between Paddington and Cardiff. The opening of the Badminton cut-off route in 1903 allowed journey times to be reduced once again and by 1907 services to and from London via the Severn Tunnel — which comprised 10 up and 12 down trains each day — had been reduced to an average journey time of about 3hr. Times were further reduced during 1912 with the introduction of the Irish Mail services to and from Fishguard which were timed to complete the distance between London and Cardiff in 2hr 50min. During the 1920s and 1930s the services were accelerated further and by 1935 the fastest journey time had

Previous page:
2-6-2T No 5574 and two autocoaches heads an SLS special over the freight-only Roath Branch on 13 July 1957.

S. Rickard

Right:
An unidentified Taff Vale 'A' class 0-6-2T speeds past Maindy Halt with the 3.50pm service from Cardiff to Merthyr in the early 1920s.

Top:
A Cardiff Clarence Road to Pontypridd service hauled by Barry Railway 'J' class 2-4-2T No 86 arrives at Cardiff Riverside station on 11 August 1913.
                          K. Nunn

Above right:
Another 'A' class, No 75, stands at Cardiff Queen Street with a valleys service in the early 1920s. Behind the locomotive is Queen Street signalbox. This was opened in 1887 but was made redundant in 1928 with the junction improvements and the construction of two new boxes.

been cut to 2hr 40min. For many years these times remained fairly static, but during the 1950s a number of named express services were introduced by the Western Region. The 'South Wales Pullman' operated between Swansea and London and was aimed particularly at businessmen. The wonderfully named 'Red Dragon' ran between Carmarthen and Paddington and the 'Pembroke Coast Express' between Paddington and Pembroke Dock. Cardiff's own service the 'Capitals United Express' was for many years during the 1950s hauled by a beautifully turned out Canton 'Castle' or 'Britannia'. The up 'Pembroke Coast Express' service was actually the fastest train of the day between London and Cardiff taking 2hr 30min to complete the 145 miles.

Steam traction was gradually withdrawn from South Wales services during the early 1960s, being replaced firstly by diesel hydraulics and later by diesel electrics. In September 1961 the steam-hauled 'South Wales Pullman' service was replaced by the new 'Blue Pullman' train with the resultant journey time being cut to 2hr 7min. The biggest change came in October 1976 when IC125 sets were introduced on South Wales services. The resulting reduction in journey

Above:
A service from Penarth enters Cardiff in about 1922 hauled by an unidentified 'A' class 0-6-2T. The large structure straddling the platforms is the luggage bridge and also in view are the three electric lifts connecting the bridge to each platform.

Opposite:
A Great Western 'Mogul' 2-6-0 runs through flood waters at Ely to the west of Cardiff on 2 November 1927.

times to about 2hr, together with the improved quality of service has seen passenger numbers increase. Today, there is an hourly shuttle service between London and Cardiff with a Pullman service once again. The 08.00 service from London Paddington to Swansea, the 'St Davids Pullman', reaches Cardiff in just 113min including stops at Reading, Bristol Parkway and Newport.

Cross Country services have been a feature of operations from Cardiff for many years. Prior to the turn of the century the Rhymney Railway operated through coaches from Cardiff to Aberystwyth, and (via LNWR lines) to Liverpool, Manchester and Crewe.

The 1896 Great Western timetable shows a through service from Cardiff to Portsmouth (a service that is still running today). By the early 1900s there were also through services to Dover, Southampton and Bournemouth, although some of these were Saturday-only trains. The north east was reached by the 'Ports to Ports Express' which was inaugurated on 2 May 1906 and ran between Barry and Newcastle via Cheltenham, Banbury and the Great Central. In later years the service operated from Swansea but in September 1939 the service was suspended. When it reappeared in October 1946 it ran via Banbury, Oxford and Swindon. A Cardiff–Newcastle service still remains a feature of the timetable but today operates via Bristol.

In 1922 one of the daily Portsmouth trains was extended to run as a restaurant express to Brighton. Apart from the war years the cross country services saw little change. In 1934 the average journey time between Cardiff and Birmingham was 4hr and Liverpool 6hr. (Today Birmingham can be reached in a little over 2hr and Liverpool in $3^1/_4$ hr.)

By the 1960s through services were running to Portsmouth, Brighton, Paignton, Penzance, Liverpool, Manchester and to Sheffield and Newcastle. This latter long-running service now ran via Birmingham although on summer Saturdays an additional service operated once again via Banbury and the Great Central main line. In 1958 services to Gloucester and Birmingham and to Hereford and Shrewsbury were operated by diesel multiple-units, and in February 1959 DMUs were also introduced on services to Bristol and Swansea. By 1965 steam had been replaced by diesel on the cross country trains, services being operated by a mixture of DMU and locomotive haulage. During the 1970s the Shrewsbury service was extended through to Crewe and was for a time hauled by Eastleigh-based Class 33 locomotives, as was the through service to and from Brighton.

Right:
Semi-streamlined Castle No 5005 Manorbier Castle stands at Cardiff General in the summer of 1935 with a service to Paddington. The streamlining was not a success and was eventually removed.
N. Ingram

Below:
Taff Vale 'A' class No 312 stands at Barry Town on Wednesday 3 June 1953 with the 2.50pm service to Bridgend.
E. Mountford

Above:
Another Taff Vale Class A, No 361 stands at Barry Pier station on 3 June 1953 with a service to Cardiff. Barry Pier was closed to passengers on 19 October 1971.

        E. Mountford

In recent years through services to the north east have been reduced to just one train a day in each direction. In 1984 there were three separate through services from Cardiff to Leeds, Newcastle and York. The current service which is operated using IC125s runs from Swansea to York. The return service, however, still starts from Newcastle.

The valley line services have always formed a major part of the passenger network in the Cardiff area, although during the early days both the Taff Vale and the Rhymney Railways were probably more interested in mineral traffic. In 1841, for example, Taff Vale passenger services comprised only two trains a day to and from Merthyr, the Rhymney being hardly better with an opening service of three a day. Gradually, however, the services increased and prior to the Grouping, the Taff Vale, Rhymney, Cardiff and Barry companies were running extensive services between Cardiff and Merthyr, Rhymney, Aberdare, Treherbert, Rhydyfelin and Barry. The opening of the short branch from Barry to Barry Island in August 1886 improved the popularity of the Island as a holiday resort. From its opening the railway generated a considerable amount of excursion traffic and for many years Barry Island was known as the Blackpool of Wales.

In the period prior to World War 1 Cardiff Riverside station alone was handling more than 100 Barry Railway and Taff Vale trains each weekday, many of which were railmotor services. The Taff Vale had introduced railmotors on to many of its services during 1904, operating between Cardiff and Pontypridd, Penarth, Cadoxton and Maindy. This latter 'business' service ran from Bute Road to Maindy calling *en route* at Queen Street and Cathays Halt. From 1 March 1911 the Cardiff Railway also operated a railmotor service from Cardiff Parade to Rydyfelin. Both the Taff Vale and Cardiff Railway railmotor services were replaced after World War 1 with autotrains.

continued on page 31

Above:
The 1pm service from Barry Island to Cardiff Queen Street departs from Barry Island on 5 September 1954 behind ex-Great Western 0-6-2T No 5601. Today the 20min interval service to Cardiff is operated using just one platform.
E. Mountford

Right:
The up 'Red Dragon' the 7.30am service from Carmarthen to Paddington hauled by 'Britannia' No 70026 Polar Star, approaches St Mellons West signalbox to the east of Cardiff on 1 June 1953.
S. Rickard

Above:
A pair of beautifully turned out Canton-allocated 'Castles' Nos 5006 Tregenna Castle and 5080 Defiant are seen here entering Cardiff General on 9 July 1953 with the return Royal Train working to London.
E. Mountford

Right:
'4500' class 2-6-2T No 4589 departs from Cardiff Queen Street on 6 October 1953 with a service from Coryton to Cardiff Bute Road. The two coaches are ex-Taff Vale trailers Nos 6 and 53.
S. Rickard

Below right:
The 1.0pm service from Gloucester to Cardiff passes Rumney, east of Cardiff on 22 April 1954, hauled by BR Standard Class 4 No 75009.
S. Rickard

Above:
The auto service to Cardiff Bute Road stands at Coryton halt in the charge of 2-6-2T No 5568 in May 1954. The northern section of this ex-Cardiff Railway branch from Coryton to Rhydyfelin was closed to passenger traffic on 20 July 1931.
Real Photos

Right:
GWR 0-6-2T No 6622 emerges from Caerphilly Tunnel as it approaches Cefn-On halt with the 1.34pm service from Aberdare (High Level) to Cardiff Queen Street on Saturday 31 July 1954.
E. Mountford

Below right:
0-6-2T No 5680 on the 3.15pm service from Cardiff Queen Street to Quakers Yard approaches Cefn-On halt on 31 July 1954. The now closed Tunnel South signalbox can just be seen behind the locomotive.
E. Mountford

Right:
'Hall' class 4-6-0 No 5925 Eastcote Hall accelerates away from Cardiff past the old carriage shed at Canton with a service to Swansea on 21 August 1955.
D. Penney

Below right:
'Castle' class No 4073 Caerphilly Castle hauls the 4.45pm service from Cardiff to Paddington past Pengam Junction Cardiff on Sunday 2 June 1957. The train is being diverted from the up main to the up relief lines due to engineering work. On the left is the Roath Dock branch.
R. O. Tuck

Below:
The 12.57pm service from Cardiff to Cadoxton hauled by 0-6-2T No 5627 approaches Dingle Road halt (Penarth) on 20 February 1957. The halt was opened as Dingle Road Platform on 1 March 1904 and was renamed Dingle Road Halt by the GWR on 2 October 1922.
R. O. Tuck

Right:
The 4.55pm service from Barry to Pontypridd hauled by 2-6-2T No 5527 calls at Wenvoe on the original Barry Railway main line on 6 August 1957. The line and station were closed to passengers on 10 September 1962.
                    Ian L. Wright

Below right:
A sad occasion as specially cleaned ex-Taff Vale 'A' class No 373 (TV No 139) arrives at Queen Street on 5 June 1957 with the 1.34pm service from Merthyr to Cardiff. This was the final occasion that an ex-Taff Vale engine appeared on a valley line passenger service.
                    E. Mountford

Below:
GWR 'City' class 4-4-0 No 3440 City of Truro departs from Cardiff on 18 May 1957 with a return Ian Allan Locospotters Club special.

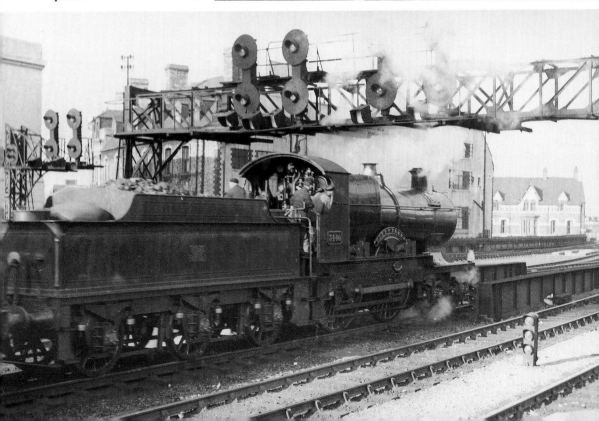

Above:
BR Standard 2-6-2T No 82043 enters Cardiff Central on 7 October 1957 with the 12.35 service from Cardiff Queen Street to Barry. A number of these locomotives were allocated to Barry in the 1950s specifically to work these trains.
      E. Mountford

Right:
GWR 2-6-2T No 4163 having just departed from Grangetown station approaches Penarth South Curve on 26 January 1958 with a service to Cardiff.
      R. O. Tuck

Below right:
The 9.13am service from Penarth hauled by 0-6-0PT No 6435, enters Clarence Road station on 7 March 1958. At this time this was one of the few remaining local steam passenger turns as many of the services had been taken over by the newly-introduced DMUs.
      R. O. Tuck

Above:
The last normal working of the auto service from Bute Road to Cathays and Maindy Halt, the 12.06 pm service from Bute Road, is seen entering Queen Street on Saturday 28 June 1958 hauled by GWR 0-6-0PT No 6435.
                    E. Mountford

Right:
On the same day the 12.47 pm return service from Maindy Halt to Bute Road again hauled by 0-6-0PT No 6435 with auto second No 458 and trailer car No 177 passes Woodville Road halt en route to Cardiff. Woodville Road was opened on 2 July 1906 and closed on 15 September 1958.
                    E. Mountford

Below right:
'Britannia' 462 No 70016 Ariel departs from Cardiff on Saturday 19 July 1958 with the 12.38pm service from Cardiff to Manchester. The 15 Western Region 'Britannia' locomotives were all allocated to Canton at this time, being used on cross country services and also main line services to and from Paddington.

On 8 May 1922 the Great Western formed the Cardiff Valleys Division to co-ordinate both passenger and goods workings over the formerly independent valley lines. One immediate effect for passengers was the construction of a new junction, just to the north of Queen Street, between the Rhymney and Taff Vale lines, and the closure of the old Parade station. Once this was completed all the former Rhymney and Cardiff Railway traffic was switched into a newly enlarged Queen Street, thus allowing former Rhymney and Cardiff Railway services to work through to Bute Road, Cardiff General, Penarth and Barry. Within a year of opening, the new station at Queen Street was handling over 300 trains a day (the figure in 1910 was 192).

In 1931 the former Cardiff Railway service between Coryton and Rhydyfelin was withdrawn, with services from Cardiff terminating at Coryton. Apart from the odd fluctuation, valley line services remained relatively unchanged until 1953 when for the start of the winter timetable in September a 'regular interval' service of push-pull trains was introduced on to the valley services by the Western Region. The reduction in time caused by the locomotive having to 'run round' its train speeded up services. However, in 1957 the first of the diesel **multiple-units were introduced to Valley line services. The**

Right:
The 9.13am service from Penarth to Cardiff Clarence Road hauled by 0-6-0PT No 6435 coasts nonstop through Penarth Dock station on 20 October 1958. Penarth Dock was closed to passengers on 1 January 1962.

R. O. Tuck

Below right:
The new order at Cardiff Queen Street in September 1958 with from left to right DMU services from Barry Island to Merthyr, Treherbert to Barry Island and from Rhymney to Penarth.

J. Hodge

first units operated from Cardiff to Treherbert on 11 September 1957, to Barry on 14 October 1957 and to Rhymney on 16 October 1957 with full services being operated between Barry and Treherbert from 13 January 1958 and from Cardiff to Rhymney from 21 April 1958. By 1960 steam traction had all but disappeared from valley line passenger services. In the late 1950s Clarence Road was being used by about 30 trains a day to Barry, Penarth, and Pontypridd via St Fagans. Bute Road which served the dock area had about 38 trains daily mainly to and from the Rhondda and Rhymney Valleys. However this figure was drastically reduced by the withdrawal of the Bute Road-Maindy autotrain service from 15 September 1958. Passenger services were withdrawn from Clarence Road and Cardiff Riverside on 16 March 1964. The general rundown of valley services from Cardiff also saw passenger services to both Aberdare and Maerdy withdrawn on 15 June 1964. It is interesting to reflect that of the 59 branch lines in South Wales that were operational in 1970, only 11 are still currently open. However, in 1971 many of the remaining valley line stations were modernised and with the introduction of ticket issuing on trains a small but significant resurgence of valley line services took place. This has culminated in the introduction of new trains and the **introduction of services to Aberdare and Maesteg.**

Below:
A view of Penarth Dock station on Saturday 30 December 1961 — the last day of passenger services over the line. Standing at the platform is the 1.55pm service from Penarth to Cardiff General, the last train to call at the station.
E. Mountford

Right:
A Barry Island to Merthyr service comprised of a pair of three-car DMU sets stands at Dinas Powis station on 27 July 1963.

Below:
Single car unit No W55019 waits at Cadoxton with an afternoon service to Penarth via Lavenock and Sully in March 1968. This route from Barry to Cardiff was closed to passengers on 6 May 1958.

R E. Masterman

Right:
A Class 119 cross-country set stands at Cardiff General on 18 April 1970 with a service to Bristol.
D. Birch

Below:
The 17.38 service from Bute Road to Coryton stands in the now disused platform at Bute Road on 22 February 1971. Services today use the platform on the right.
M. C. Barker

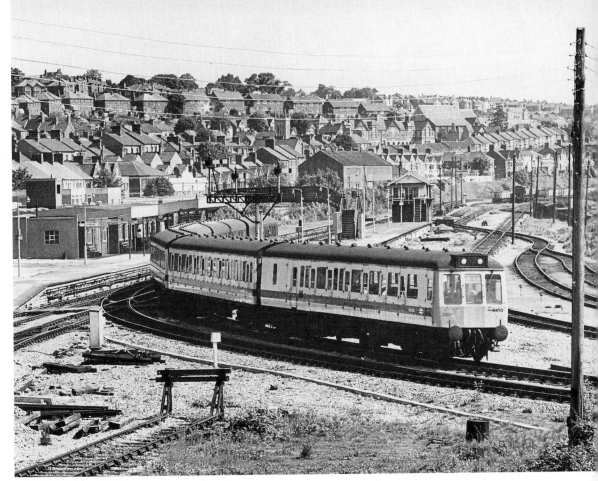

Above:
A six-car DMU set comprising Swindon and Derby units departs from Barry Town on Sunday 11 June 1978 with the 10.05 service from Cardiff Central to Barry Island.
L. Bertram

Right:
A Class 116 unit arrives at Radyr on Saturday 18 April 1981 with a service from Queen Street to Treherbert. On the right is the entrance to the large yard and on the left Radyr Junction signalbox.
B. Edwards

Opposite:
A Barry to Treherbert service stands at the newly opened station at Cathays on 3 October 1983. This was the first completely new station to be opened in the Cardiff area under the BR/County Council initiative.

Hills Welsh Press

Above:
The driver of a Class 116 DMU on the 13.00 service from Coryton to Bute Road exchanges tokens at Heath Junction on 21 February 1981.

Dr J. McGregor

Right:
'Heritage' set C395 stands at Bute Road station on 27 April 1990 with the shuttle service to Queen Street. The row of preserved locomotives standing in the disused Platform 2 have since been moved elsewhere.

Kevin Lane

Above:
In the days when some of the cross-country services to and
from Cardiff were locomotive-hauled, Class 37 No
37431 stands at Cardiff Central on 16 December 1988
with the 15.55 service to Liverpool Lime Street. Today
these services are worked using Class 158 units.

M. Jones

CHAPTER 3
Goods
Services

Goods services have always formed an important part of railway operations at Cardiff and as the description of this traffic could fill a book on its own, one can but summarise the main features.

Such was the importance placed on the traffic of coal, iron ore and other commodities to the docks, that many of the companies considered it to be of greater importance than their passenger traffic. Around the turn of the century the Taff Vale Railway alone was operating some 250 general goods, mineral and empty wagon trains each day. To cope with the large amounts of coal and other goods a number of very large marshalling yards and wagon storage sidings were opened in the Cardiff area both in the docks, and also at Newtown, Roath, Canton and Radyr. After the Grouping the Great Western centralised all of these goods services with the formation of the Cardiff Valleys Division. The control office was for many years situated at Cardiff Queen Street and to cope with the traffic the Division was essentially divided into three sections: the Taff Vale, the Rhymney and the Barry. The withdrawal of steam traction and the gradual reduction in the use of coal for both domestic and industrial purposes saw the coal trade diminish as one by one the mines in the valleys have closed. This has resulted in the closure of almost all of these yards and Radyr, the last of the big pre-Grouping yards, was closed during 1993.

Previous page:
A wartime shot taken on 12 May 1943 shows coal traffic at Radyr yard. On the right is a Great Western Mogul and in the centre an ex-Taff Vale 'A' class tank.
British Rail

Opposite:
A Rhymney Railway Class
A 0-6-2T No 115 passes
Heath Junction at Cardiff
with a down coal train on
11 August 1913.
                    Ken Nunn

Above:
A down train of coal
empties approaches Llandaff
hauled by ex-Taff Vale
Class A No 410 (18) on 31
March 1923.
                    Ken Nunn

Right:
'Aberdare' class 2-6-0
No 2656 runs through
Cardiff General on 15 May
1943 with an up steel train.

Of the pre-Grouping companies, the Taff Vale's goods station was situated adjacent to its Queen Street station. The Rhymney operated goods depots at both Salisbury Road and, from 1871, at its old passenger station at Adam Street. The London & North Western also operated its own goods depot in the docks at Tyndall Street. The main Great Western goods depot at Cardiff was situated to the east of the station at Newtown. The original South Wales Railway goods station was next to the passenger station but it was moved to Newtown in 1872. Newtown goods was enlarged in 1889 with the addition of a new shed and it was here that most of the general goods traffic was dealt with. Such was the growth of this traffic that in 1910 the GWR extended the buildings and yard once again. Adjacent to the goods station were the horse stables.

continued on page 48

Above:
Some idea of the vast yards that were constructed by each of the companies to deal with the coal traffic can be seen in this 1920s picture of the ex-Barry Railway coal storage sidings at Cadoxton North.

Right:
'5600' class 0-6-2T No 6665 restarts an empty coal train at Heath Junction Cardiff on 9 February 1952.
Brian Williams

Below right:
0-6-0PT No 9677 shunts in the now closed yard at Pengam (to the east of Cardiff) on 1 February 1953.
S. Rickard

Right:
Another view of Pengam taken on 24 January 1954 shows Taff Vale '04' class 0-6-2T No 215 (118) on shunting duty.

S. Rickard

Below right:
Another shot of Rhymney Class R1 No 38 as it leaves Cardiff Docks with a short freight on Saturday 5 October 1957. This was the very last working for an ex-Rhymney Railway locomotive.

E. Mountford

Below:
Ex-Rhymney Railway Class R1 0-6-2T No 38 makes a fine sight as it passes Cherry Orchard sidings with a down goods on 27 September 1957, just two weeks before withdrawal.

E. Mountford

44

Right:
The east end of Cardiff General on Monday 7 October 1957 shows 0-6-0PT No 5787 on an up goods as it waits for 'Castle' class No 5048 Earl of Devon to depart on the 12.32pm service to Exeter.

Below right:
A down goods hauled by a '5600' class 0-6-2T on the ex-Barry Railway Tonteg Junction to Cadoxton line crosses the South Wales main line near St Fagans on 20 February 1959.
*   S. Rickard*

Bottom right:
'5600' class 0-6-2T No 5631 runs through Cardiff General with an up goods in the early 1960s. The 5600 and 6600s were constructed by the Great Western in the 1920s to replace many of the older types inherited by the company after the Grouping. They saw much service over the valley lines right up until the end of steam traction.
*   R. H. G. Simpson*

Below:
Standard Class 5 No 73018 enters Cardiff General on 18 July 1958 with the 5.15pm Whitland to Kensington milk service.
*   R. O. Tuck*

Right:
Locomotive change at Canton on 10 February 1977 as Class 47 No 47378 leaves charge of an up tanker train to fellow class member No 47204 seen waiting in the siding.
G. Pinder

Below right:
Class 46 No 163 Leicestershire and Derbyshire Yeomanry enters Cardiff Central from the west with an up goods service on 5 June 1973.
Norman Preedy

Below:
Class 25s Nos 7516 and 7504 round the curve at the east end of Cardiff Central on 5 June 1973 with down coal empties.
Norman Preedy

Above:
Busy time at Radyr on 5 April 1978 as Class 37 No 37281 and '08' No 08195 wait in the sidings as Class 116 set C320 arrives at the station with a Cardiff to Treherbert service.
M. Rhodes

Right:
Class 37 No D6772 shunts ore wagons at Grangetown Ore Sidings prior to taking the 9.15am Saturdays only empties from Grangetown to Redmire on 16 July 1966.
L. Sandler

Right:
Another pair of Class 37s, Nos 37154 and 37162, pass through Queen Street station on 6 February 1986 with an MGR train from Tower Colliery to Aberthaw power station.
Ian Allan Library

Right:
Double-headed coal trains on the Valley lines are now almost a thing of the past. Here in better days a pair of Class 37s Nos 37270 and 37333 run down through Radyr with a Tower Colliery to Aberthaw MGR working on 21 May 1981.
Les Bertram

Below:
Class 56 Nos 56045 and 56041 head the 12.05 service from Llanwern to Port Talbot Docks past Pengam Freightliner terminal on 22 July 1983. The terminal site may be used for Channel Tunnel traffic.
Paul D. Shannon

Horses were used for delivery purposes and according to Great Western records there were more than 100 located at the Newtown Goods stables in 1910. At this time the Great Western goods staff at Newtown numbered nearly 500. Some idea of just how busy this depot was is shown by the fact that some 40 trains called each day whilst another 112 originated or terminated at Newtown with services to and from London, Birmingham, Birkenhead, West Wales and the West of England. The equally important parcels department was originally situated on Platforms 1 (outward parcels) and 6 (inward parcels) at the GWR station and in 1910 was dealing with more than 500,000 parcels a year. In 1934 with annual parcels figures over the million mark a new parcels department was built by the Great Western on the south side of the station. During the same year the old carriage shed at Canton was converted into a milk and fruit depot. The depot was eventually used by National Carriers but in recent years it has been used as an Isis Link depot. Newtown goods was also taken over by National Carriers, but has now been closed for a number of years. Today the old parcels building at the station lies derelict and awaiting demolition.

Since 1987 freight in the area has been operated under the Railfreight banner, with trainload services by the Coal, Petroleum, Metal and Construction sub-Sectors, and (until 1990) Speedlink wagonload freight by Railfreight Distribution. The reorganisation of the trainload services under three regionally-based companies saw freight in the Cardiff area come largely under Trainload Freight West, which has now been reincorporated as Transrail.

It does seem incredible that today much of the coal traffic passing through Cardiff is not Welsh but imported from overseas via Port Talbot and Avonmouth docks.

Above:
Class 37 No 37895 runs through Barry on 16 August 1993 with an empty MGR service from Aberthaw to Tower Colliery. Since this picture was taken Tower Colliery has been closed by British Coal and subsequently purchased and operated by its employees.
Author

CHAPTER 4
Locomotive Depots

With a number of smaller railway companies as well as the GWR running into the city it is not surprising that each provided its own locomotive servicing facilities. These ranged in size from single-road depots right up to a depot such as Cardiff Canton which was (and still is) the largest locomotive depot in the principality.

The first locomotive shed in Cardiff was opened by the Taff Vale Railway at West Yard in 1840. This small single-road shed was soon found to be inadequate and was replaced in 1845 by a new shed situated adjacent to the terminus at Bute Street. The old shed saw further use first as a carriage repair shed and later as an engineering shop. The new two-road building which was known as the Terminus Shed was constructed of timber but an increase in the company's motive power saw the shed extended in 1847 and again in 1849, and it is highly probable that it was during this latter extension that the timber sides were replaced by stone. The shed itself was situated between the dock lines and Bute Street which made further extension impossible. So in 1857 the company constructed a new six-road shed just to the south of the original depot which was subsequently converted into a carriage shed. The new terminus shed was constructed of stone and remained in use until 1884 when the company opened a new and very much larger depot at Cathays. The six-road depot was subsequently demolished to make way for the new Rhymney Railway 'Docks' (later Bute Street) station.

Previous page:
The interior of Cardiff East Dock on 6 January 1932. The shed had opened just a few weeks previously.

Opposite:
An LNWR Webb Coal Tank
0-6-2T, No 3739, together
with Rhymney Railway 'L'
class 2-4-2ST No 1324 (ex
RR No 65) stands in the
yard at the old Rhymney
Railway shed at Cardiff
Docks on 7 August 1924.
The shed was closed in
1931 with the opening by
the Great Western of its new
shed at East Dock.

Top:
Another view of Cardiff
Docks taken on 1 May
1927. From left to right are
Barry Railway Class F
0-6-0ST No 708 (No 37)
and Class B No 211 (No
17) and Cardiff Railway
Kitson 0-6-2T No 161
(No 21).
H. C. Casserley

Above right:
Cardiff Cathays was opened
by the Taff Vale in 1884.
This photograph is dated
1885 and shows Taff Vale
2-4-0 No 22 (built in 1863)
standing in the yard at
Cathays.

This new Taff Vale shed at Cathays contained 10 roads and was the largest on the Taff Vale system. In fact, in terms of engine movements (for much of its life its allocation comprised solely of tank locomotives), it was probably on a par with the much larger Great Western shed at Canton. The twin bays were constructed of stone with a glazed roof. Sometime around 1939 the east bay was shortened to form open sidings and a five-road repair shop. Cathays lost its main shed status as far as steam was concerned when in December 1957 it officially became a sub-shed of Radyr. The introduction of DMUs onto some valley services in October 1957 saw the main building converted into a DMU depot and in July 1958 the shed was officially closed to steam. With the construction of the new diesel depot at Canton, Cathays became redundant and was finally closed in November 1964.

The Taff Vale also operated a small shed five miles to the north of the city at Radyr. The depot, which up until about 1914 was known as Penarth Junction, was opened in 1865 and probably replaced an earlier but smaller shed on the same site. This small two-road timber shed was situated in the goods yard adjacent to Radyr station and was closed in March 1931 with the opening of the new depot to the south of Radyr Yard.

The new depot was constructed by the Great Western under the 1929 Loans Act and was opened on 29 March 1931. The building was a standard 'loan' type four-road straight shed. Originally a sub-shed of Cathays, it became the main depot with the partial closure of Cathays in December 1957. The shed was never fully dieselised and was closed completely in July 1965. For a number of years the building was used by an engineering company and by 1994 was standing derelict amidst the remnants of the now closed Radyr yard.

Cardiff Bute Yard shed was situated on an area of land between the East and West Docks. The shed, which was also known as Tyndall Street, was opened by The Marquis of Bute's Trustees (later Bute Docks Co) in April 1862. The two-road stone built depot had an allocation of about 20 tank locomotives. The shed was closed in 1881 when a new depot was opened on the other side of the east dock at East Moors. The old Bute Yard building was however retained in use as part of the company's main workshop.

Below right:
A fine view of Cathays on 8 August 1924 , in view from left to right are former Taff Vale engines Nos 346 ('A' class No 45), 296 ('O4' class No 94), 444 ('M1' class No 14), 420 ('O4' class No 69), 384 ('A' class No 164), 364 ('A' class No 129) and 380 ('A' class No 158).

Below:
An official photograph of the new coaling stage at Cathays dated 8 October 1931 shows Nos 723 (Barry Railway Class F No 103) and No 208 (Barry Railway Class B No 14) together with an unidentified '5600' class 062T. British Rail

Above:
A view of Cardiff Cathays taken on 4 September 1955 shows '5101' class 2-6-2T Nos 4161 and 4163, Taff Vale 'A' class 0-6-2T No 362 and '5600' class 0-6-2T No 6665. During 1957 the shed became a sub-shed of Radyr.

East Moors was opened by the Bute Docks Company in August 1881 and was altogether a much larger facility. The new shed contained six roads and was constructed of brick with a slated roof. With the Grouping came a certain amount of rationalisation of some of the older locomotive sheds and on 8 March 1926 East Moors was closed by the GWR; its allocation of about 30 locomotives were transferred to the nearby ex-Rhymney shed at Cardiff Docks.

Cardiff Docks had been opened by the Rhymney Railway in October 1857. The original shed which was constructed of stone with a timber roof contained four roads, but records show that it was extended in length some time around 1873. The locomotive accommodation was further extended during 1901 when locomotive repairs were switched to the new works at Caerphilly and carriage repairs to Cathays, and the locomotive and carriage works at Cardiff Docks became part of the shed complex. In 1930 the Great Western demolished the old works buildings and, under the 1929 Loans Act, constructed a new eight-road shed. Cardiff East Dock as it was known was opened on 19 January 1931 after which the original Rhymney Railway four-road shed was closed and demolished. The new shed had an allocation of about 70 locomotives. Cardiff East Dock was eventually closed to steam on 8 March 1958 but was retained as a stabling point for Class 08 dock shunters. On 10 September 1962 the nearby shed at Cardiff Canton was closed for conversion into a diesel depot and from that date East Dock was reopened to service the displaced steam locomotives. The reactivated East Dock was finally closed on 2 August 1965 with the withdrawal of steam traction from the Docks and Valley lines and the transfer of the '08s' to Canton.

Although the broad gauge South Wales Railway opened its line from Chepstow to Swansea on 18 June 1850, the company did not open an engine shed at Cardiff until December 1858. The shed was situated on the down side of the main line at Newtown and just to the east of the Bute Docks Junction. This single-road shed was converted to standard gauge in May 1852 and it is also probable that at this time it was rebuilt into a two-road depot. It remained in use until May 1882 when it was replaced by the new GWR shed at Canton.

Cardiff Canton was opened in May 1882 and together with Swansea Landore is the only surviving locomotive shed in South Wales still in railway use. The shed which is situated in the triangle of lines just to the west of Central station was constructed of brick. It initially comprised a six-road straight shed but this was enlarged in 1897 with the addition of a large roundhouse building. Various alterations over the years saw a new fitting and lifting shop added in 1925 and in 1934 facilities were again improved with the addition of a new coaling plant and a 65ft turntable. At the same time a new 810ft-long carriage shed was constructed at Canton. The new carriage shed contained 11 tracks and had a capacity of about 150 coaches. It replaced a smaller seven-road shed which stood almost opposite but on the north side of the main line. (This shed saw further use as a depot for milk, fish and fruit, and at the time of writing is currently in use as an ISIS link Railfreight Distribution depot.)

continued on page 61

Below:
In 1958 the main shed building at Cathays was converted into a servicing depot for the new DMUs that were being introduced onto some Valley line services. This photograph dated 25 February 1959 shows part of the new DMU shop.

British Rail

Right:
A pair of Taff Vale Railway 'A' class 0-6-2Ts Nos 345 and 347 together with GWR 0-6-0PT 6436 stand in the loco yard at Cardiff Cathays on 23 August 1953.

Below right:
Another view of Cardiff East Dock, taken on 16 March 1958 with four '5700' class 0-6-0PTs Nos 6751/6744/6702 and 6701. The depot was closed during the same month but was reopened again in September 1962 and used for servicing steam locomotives after Canton was closed for reconstruction into a diesel depot.

Below:
Taff Vale 0-6-2T No 36 stands in the shed yard at Cardiff East Dock on 12 May 1957. Also in view are GWR 0-6-0s Nos 6703 and 3402.

J. D. Edwards

Above:
The shed at Radyr was
constructed in 1931 under
the Loans Act. The shed is
pictured here shortly after
opening on 9 October 1931.

Right:
A later view of Radyr taken
in June 1959 shows from
left to right '3400' class
0-6-0PT No 3408, '5600'
class 0-6-2T No 6614,
'5100' class 2-6-2T No
4177, '5700' class 0-6-0PT
No 3672 and '6400' class
0-6-0PT No 6434.

Below right:
New and old at Radyr with
Class 37 diesels mingling
with GWR 5700 class
0-6-0PTs.The shed was
closed on 26 July 1965.
Hugh Ballantyne

Right:
A Taff Vale 'V' class 0-6-0ST No 791 (TVR 291) stands outside the shed at Penarth Dock on 1 May 1927.
          H. C. Casserley

Below right:
Another view of Penarth Dock taken on Sunday 1 May 1927. The centre locomotive is Barry Railway Class B 0-6-2T No 223 (Barry Railway No 23). Penarth Dock was officially closed on 13 February 1929.

Below:
The sad sight of '5600' class 0-6-2T No 5692 standing dead at Radyr on 22 July 1965. This was the last 0-6-2T to work in the Cardiff Valleys Division, on Saturday 17 July 1965.
          E. Mountford

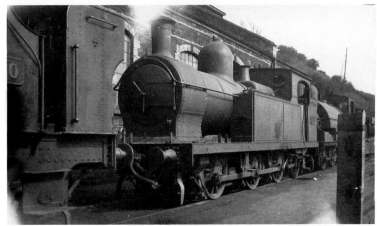

Right:
A general view of the engine shed at Barry taken on 22 September 1957.
A. R. Goult

Below right:
For many years after the end of steam traction Woodham's yard at Barry became a mecca for the steam enthusiast with up to 200 withdrawn locomotives in store. Luckily, most, if not all, of the locomotives seen here in the lower yard on 24 April 1966 have been saved.
J. Pitt

Below:
'Hall' class No 5978 Bodinnick Hall together with Castle class No 7003 Elmley Castle stand in the loco yard at Barry in 1964. After the closure of Canton shed to steam, Barry, Radyr and Cardiff East Dock became the main steam servicing depots in the Cardiff area.
D. Martin

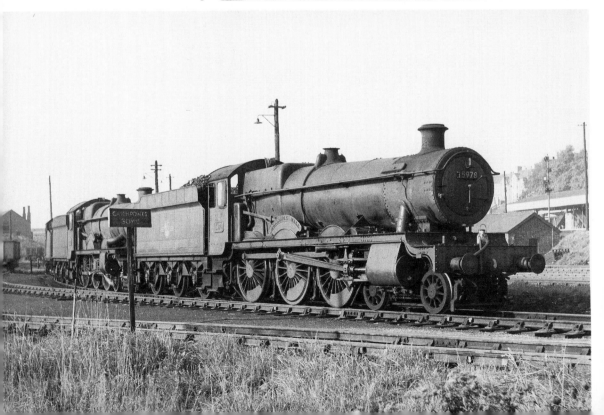

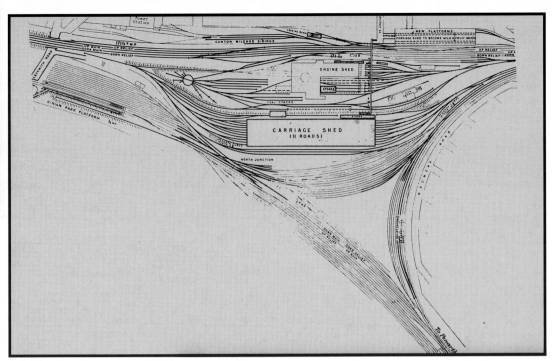

Above:
A plan of Canton taken from a 1934 Great Western Magazine shows the new carriage shed and locomotive coaling plant.

Right:
A general view of Cardiff Canton taken on 27 September 1933.

Below:
Taff Vale Class A tank No 365 (TV No 130) is pictured here on yard shunting duties at Canton in December 1954.

Above:
*A 1950s view of Canton
Loco yard. In the foreground
are Standard Class 4 No
75008, GWR '2800' class
No 2867 and 'Hall' class
No 4946 Moseley Hall.*
G. F. Heiron

Right:
*The nameplates of
'Britannias' Nos 70026
Polar Star and 70020
Mercury at Canton on
12 May 1957.*
J. D. Edwards

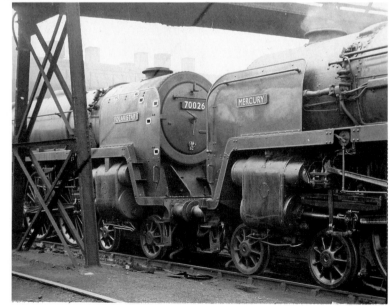

The average locomotive allocation at Canton over the years was about 120, comprising a mixture of shunting, goods and main line types. Under the Western Region modernisation plan Canton was chosen for conversion into a diesel depot. To allow conversion to take place the depot was closed on 10 September 1962, locomotives being transferred to East Dock shed. The new diesel depot,which cost £1¹/₄ million to construct, was officially opened on 18 September 1964. It covered an area of about 30 acres and was one of the four chief WR diesel locomotive maintenance depots constructed under the modernisation scheme. Although most of the old steam depot was swept away, part of the original 1882 straight shed was retained and converted into a three-road servicing shed. (This was actually the first part of the new depot to be completed, opening on 10 October 1963.) The heavy maintenance building, which can accommodate up to 16 locomotives, was built on the site of the old roundhouse. At the same time the 1934 carriage shed was modernised to deal with the servicing and maintenance of DMUs.

Right:
'Castle' class 4-6-0 No 5057 Earl Waldegrave stands in the loco yard at Canton in June 1960.
Author's Collection

Below:
A official view of the new diesel repair shop depot at Canton. The depot was opened on 18 September 1964, and in this picture Class 35, 47 and 52 locomotives are under repair.
British Rail

It is interesting to reflect that the official BR handout at the time states that the new diesel depot was responsible for the maintenance of 62 shunters, 41 diesel hydraulics, 317 diesel electrics and 96 multiple unit sets (the official allocation at the time is shown as just 121 locomotives). Today, Canton is the only servicing and maintenance depot in the Wales, dealing with Transrail freight and shunting locomotives which currently comprise Classes 08, 37, 56 and 60. Main line passenger services to and from Paddington are now exclusively operated by IC125 sets which since July 1994 are serviced overnight at the InterCity depot at Landore.

Above:
An IC125 set undergoes its final check at Canton Carriage shed prior to working an afternoon service to Paddington on 26 November 1980. Today IC125 sets used on Swansea and Cardiff trains are serviced at Landore.
R. E Masterman

Two other locomotive sheds deserve a mention as both were situated within a few miles of the city. The first, Penarth Dock, stood adjacent to Penarth Dock station. It was constructed in stone by the Taff Vale Railway in 1887, and contained three roads. Over the years the depot had an allocation of around 20 tank engines. Gradually its work was switched to nearby Barry and the shed was officially closed on 13 February 1929 although records show that it continued to be used until 22 October of the same year.

Just eight miles south of Cardiff is the small coastal town of Barry, and it was here in 1890 that the Barry Railway company opened its own locomotive depot. The shed was constructed of brick and contained six through roads. In 1925 the GWR undertook some improvements which included the provision of a new coaling plant. During the 1930s the shed allocation comprised solely of tank types which rendered the turntable surplus to requirements and it was removed by the Great Western. During the mid-1950s the Western Region replaced the original shed roof with a new corrugated structure. Barry was closed to steam in September 1964 but the main building is still essentially intact and at the time of writing is being used as a repair and maintenance depot for merry-go-round coal wagons.

CHAPTER 5
Cardiff
General

A small station was opened on the site of the present Central station by the South Wales Railway on 18 June 1850. Early plans show that although there were four through tracks, the station comprised an up and a down platform each with its own bay. The station was enlarged during 1896, the down island platform was widened and both up and down platforms were extended in length. A second island platform (No 6) together with extra office accommodation was constructed on the down side. This now gave the station a total of six platforms with Nos 1, 3, 4 and 6 being 800ft in length. A fish bay was constructed at the west end of the new No 6 platform, and was at peak times apparently also used for passenger services. The extra platforms were primarily added to accommodate Taff Vale services that had commenced running into the GWR station, via a new connecting line from Queen Street which had been opened during the same year. The new connection was constructed as a flying junction, which allowed valley services access to the new platforms without blocking main line services. The two new platforms were also used by GWR services departing from or terminating at the station.

Previous page:
The interior of the entrance hall showing the new ticket office, again taken on 25 April 1934. Notice the wonderful 1930s-style electric lights.

Opposite:
A service from Barry hauled by Barry Railway Class G 044T No 68 arrives at Cardiff Riverside Junction Station in 1911. The station which was opened on 14 August 1893 was rebuilt in the 1930s as a single island platform.

Above:
The new station at Riverside Junction pictured here on 25 April 1934. It was not officially amalgamated into the General station, becoming Platforms 8 and 9, until 28 October 1940.

On 14 August 1893 the GWR opened a further two platforms, together with a ticket office, on the adjacent Riverside branch, to accommodate Taff Vale and Barry Railway services that had commenced running into Cardiff. The Riverside branch was opened by the GWR on 14 September 1882 to serve the various wharves and warehouses of the Glamorganshire Canal Company. The branch left the main line adjacent to the existing Cardiff station, from where it continued southwards for approximately a mile to terminate at Clarence Road. On 2 April 1894 passenger services were extended along the branch to Clarence Road and it was here during May 1894 that the GWR erected a single platform station to accommodate the new services. Rather surprisingly the two new platforms at Cardiff were designated Cardiff Riverside Junction and were not incorporated into the existing GWR station until 28 October 1940. The main station at Cardiff became very busy and in 1910 the station staff numbered 231.

During 1931 a start was made on the reconstruction of Cardiff General (the suffix 'General' had been added to the name in 1922). The work which cost £820,000 involved the reconstruction of the station concourse, the lengthening of the four existing main line platforms to 1,000ft and the reconstruction of the old Taff Vale platform to give two 800ft-long platforms. At the same time the old Riverside station was also rebuilt as an island platform, with two faces each 600ft-long. Other major engineering work saw the Taff River bridge widened from 78ft to 175ft which in turn allowed the main approach lines to the station to be quadrupled. In fact 18 bridges were eventually reconstructed in the course of the work.

continued on page 69

Above:
A view of the single platform station at Cardiff Clarence Road on 3 December 1958. The station, which stood at the end of the short Riverside Branch, was opened by the Great Western in 1894 when passenger services were extended along the branch. The facilities were certainly basic and as can be seen in this shot were in later years in a pretty run down state. Clarence Road was finally closed to passengers on 16 March 1964.

Above right:
GWR 0-6-0PT No 6423 stands at Clarence Road with a service to Penarth in May 1954.

Real Photos

Right:
The up departure platform at Cardiff around the turn of the century. Notice the nameboard 'Cardiff' — the station was not given the suffix 'General' until 1922.

Above:
A view of Platforms 4 and 6 in 1911. The service arriving behind a pair of 4-4-0 locomotives is almost certainly a Fishguard boat train.

Right:
A high level view of Cardiff General taken on 7 January 1931 and shortly before the reconstruction of the station. In the foreground is the west end bay (Platform 5).

Below right:
A plan of Cardiff General and Riverside stations dated 1910.

Courtesy Railway
Magazine

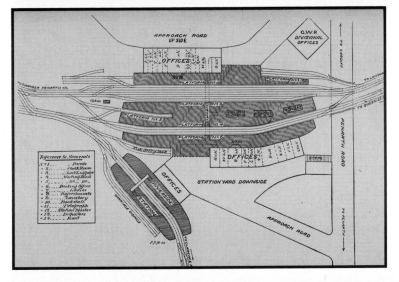

68

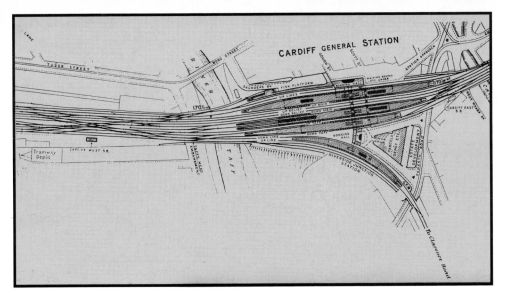

Above:
A plan of Cardiff General after the 1934 alterations.

Right:
The main entrance and booking office building at Cardiff General taken on 25 April 1934, shortly after completion.

The construction of the station concourse also saw the road level lowered by about 12ft to subway level. A new station entrance building, faced with natural Portland stone with a Cornish granite plinth, together with a new 16ft-wide subway were constructed. The former passenger subway was retained solely for luggage purposes and was connected to the platforms by new lifts. This allowed the old luggage bridge at the west end of the station to be removed. To finish off the work, colour light signalling was installed together with new all-electric boxes at the east and west ends of the station. The East box which was opened first contained 153 levers, the West box was the larger of the two and contained 339 levers. The new station was opened by the then Minister of Transport, the Hon Oliver Stanley on 26 February 1934.

In this guise the station remained relatively unchanged until the Riverside branch platforms were closed to passengers on 16 March 1964, although they continued to be used for a number of years for parcels traffic. On 7 May 1973 the station underwent a name change when the 'General' suffix was dropped and replaced with 'Central'. Some modernisation work took place during the spring of 1975 when the three small buffets situated on each of the main platforms were extended by about 25ft and converted into combined buffet and waiting rooms. On 12 July 1982 work started on the modernisation of the station concourse. The work entailed the provision of an enlarged travel centre, a new ticket office, shop unit and refreshment kiosk. Outside, the 1934 pediment declaring 'Great Western Railway' was made a feature of the refurbished entrance. The project which cost approximately £1.2 million was officially opened by Viscount Tonypandy on 16 January 1984.

Above:
New layout of the main entrance to General station after the 1930s rebuilding work can be seen to good effect in this picture of the station entrance, taken on 5 August 1960, suitably decorated for the Royal Eisteddfod.

Right:
An aerial view of Cardiff Central taken on 23 March 1972. In the foreground is the River Taff, on the upper right is Bute West Dock.
Mike Woodward

CHAPTER 6
Cardiff
Queen Street

The evolution of Cardiff Queen Street can be traced back to the first station in Cardiff, opened by the Taff Vale Railway in October 1840. The original station which was known as Cardiff Taff Vale was situated adjacent to the site of the current Queen Street Station. It had one platform at first but a second was constructed in 1862 and at the same time the headquarters of the railway were moved from the docks to new offices nearby. In 1887 the Taff Vale station was demolished, and replaced by a new station which was named Cardiff Queen Street. The new station contained two platforms and a bay at the south end, each covered by a large overall roof. In 1928 the station was enlarged to five platforms, with the addition of a new island platform on the up side to accommodate the Rhymney Railway services that had been switched from the nearby Rhymney station at Parade. Goods facilities were withdrawn from Queen Street on 1 April 1925.

Previous page:
During the autumn of 1928 Cardiff Bute Road was rebuilt by the GWR as a single island platform. This official view of the rebuilt station was taken on 19 March 1929 and shows the new layout.

Opposite above:
The main entrance to the
Taff Vale station at Cardiff
taken in April 1886 one
month before demolition.
This was the first station to
be opened in Cardiff. The
original 1840 building with
smoke vent is at the rear.
This entrance was closed
during May 1882.

Opposite below:
An up service hauled by Taff
Vale 4-4-0T No 69 waits at
Cardiff (Taff Vale) in about
1886. This platform and
building date from around
1857 when the Taff Vale
main line between Cardiff
and Merthyr was doubled.

Above:
Another view of the old Taff
Vale station in April 1886.
It was demolished during
May of the same year to
make way for the new
Queen Street station. On the
right is the main platform,
in the centre is the original
platform and train shed
which dates from the
opening of the line in 1840.
The building on the left is
the original goods shed.

The Rhymney Railway originally built its own terminus
station at Adam Street (just to the east of Queen Street) but
this was closed to passengers on 1 April 1871 when services
were moved to a new station at Cardiff Crockherbtown
(Adam Street remained open for goods traffic until 2 May
1966). The new station at Crockherbtown was situated just to
the north of the present Queen Street station and was
renamed Cardiff (Rhymney) in 1888 and Cardiff Parade in
1924 (returns for the year 1920 show that some 800,000
passengers per annum were using Parade). The station, which
comprised two through platforms and a bay, remained in use
until April 1928 when the GWR constructed the junction,
just to the north of Queen Street, linking the Taff Vale and
Rhymney lines and from 15 April 1928 Parade station was
closed completely. Queen Street remained almost unchanged
until 1973 when under the Valley lines modernisation
scheme it was rebuilt. The modernisation scheme, which cost
£³/₄ million, was started in 1971 and involved general
improvements to most of the 46 valley line stations. At this
time Queen Street was the busiest station in Wales in terms of
passenger numbers, being used by 11,000 passengers and 148
trains each weekday. Improvements at Queen Street saw the
removal of the overall roof and the station rebuilt as an
island platform with a single bay. (The bay was altered to a
through line in March 1990.) The main entrance building
was removed and replaced by a modern building housing a
new ticket office, enquiry office and bookstall. Modern
electric lifts connected the subway to the new platforms on
which a large buffet/waiting room was constructed. On the
east side of the station a large office block was constructed,
named Brunel House, and until 1984 it was the headquarters
of the Cardiff Division of the Western Region.

continued on page 78

Above:
A general view of Cardiff Queen Street station nearing completion in 1887. The new station was built on the site of the old Taff Vale station. The large roof covers the two through platform lines, whilst the smaller roof on the left covers the bay platform. Notice on the right part of the 1857 Taff Vale station building still in situ.

Above right:
The interior of the new station at Queen Street, looking south around the turn of the century.
L&GRP

Right:
Just south of Queen Street was East Branch Junction, pictured here in 1898. On the left is East Branch Box, lines to the left went to Bute Road and Bute West Dock and on the right to Cardiff General. Notice also the wonderful somersault signals.

Right:
After the Grouping Queen Street was enlarged by the Great Western and is pictured here shortly after completion on 15 May 1928, showing the two new platforms.

Right:
An interesting view of the new junction at Queen Street from the ex Rhymney station at Parade on 15 May 1928. On the left are the ex-Rhymney lines to the docks.

Right:
The wonderful entrance to Queen Street Station pictured here on 5 March 1957. Notice the pediment showing the date 1887, the year of opening.
British Rail

Right:
The Taff Vale offices at Cardiff Queen Street on 20 October 1969. The offices were subsequently demolished during station reconstruction work.
British Rail

Above:
An excellent view of the interior of Queen Street station taken in 1970, shortly before it was demolished and rebuilt.

S. Jones

Right:
The new station at Queen Street on 17 July 1975. The station is dwarfed by Brunel House, the headquarters of the one time Western Region's Cardiff Division.

Below right:
During the 1970s many of the station names were extended to include the Welsh spelling. This photo taken on 10 December 1974 shows one of the new bilingual signs. Obviously not everyone in Wales speaks the native tongue!

Bottom right:
The arrival platforms at Cardiff Parade seen here in June 1922. Parade was opened by the Rhymney Railway as Cardiff Crockherbtown on 1 April 1871. It was renamed Cardiff 'Rhymney' in November 1888 and Cardiff Parade on 1 July 1924. The station was closed to passengers on 15 April 1928 when services were diverted into Queen Street.

P. Rutherford

Right:
The entrance to Cardiff Parade station pictured here in June 1922.
P. Rutherford

Below right:
Another shot shows the departure platform at Cardiff Parade in June 1922. As can be seen this was a bay platform. The two through platforms are on the right of the picture.
P. Rutherford

Below:
This interesting picture shows the close proximity of Parade and Queen Street stations. The view again taken in June 1922 is from south end of the arrival platform at Cardiff Parade and shows, in the centre background, the ex-Taff Vale station at Cardiff Queen Street.
P. Rutherford

Cardiff Docks station was opened by the Taff Vale Railway around 1882. The station comprised two platforms connected by a footbridge and was situated alongside what was then Bute Street. It does appear that there may well have been an earlier but unofficial platform on this site. Permission to construct the docks station described here was not forthcoming until about 1879. The Great Western renamed the station Bute Street on 1 July 1924 and in 1928 the station was rebuilt by the GWR as a single island platform. During the late 1960s the station canopy together with many of the platform facilities were removed. On 22 March 1965 the station was closed to goods traffic and on 2 February 1970 Bute Road (as it had become) was reduced to an unstaffed halt. The original Taff Vale station building, which is Grade II listed, has in recent years been used as a museum. Today only one platform is in use and from the start of the winter 1994 timetable the station has been designated Cardiff Bay.

Right:
The Taff Vale station at Cardiff Docks pictured here in the early 1920s. The station which was situated alongside the Bute Road, was constructed in around 1882. The Great Western renamed the station Cardiff Bute Road on 1 July 1924.

Below:
A view of the new platform at Cardiff Bute Road looking north, taken on 19 March 1929.

CHAPTER 7
Cardiff Today

I

n recent years the railway at Cardiff has seen a resurgence in use that has probably not been matched anywhere else in the country. This has been due in no small way to the co-operation between the railway and the Mid- and South Glamorgan County councils in providing a massive investment in the railway locally and the Valley Lines in particular. The new Valley Line services were officially launched at Pontypridd on 2 February 1985. The first new station at Cardiff for almost 40 years was opened at Cathays on 3 October 1983 and from 5 October 1987 a new City Line passenger service was introduced between Radyr and Cardiff. This operates via the previously freight-only line between Radyr and Penarth North Junction, with new stations being opened at Ninian Park, Waun-gron Park, Fairwater and Danescourt. The original Great Western halt at Ninian Park was opened on 2 November 1912. It was rebuilt in 1933 but was officially closed to regular services from 10 September 1939. Fortunately, the platforms were not removed and after the war saw regular use for football traffic.

On 3 October 1988 passenger services were reinstated

Previous page:
On Monday 4 November 1985 the old halt at Cefn-On was closed and replaced by a new station at Lisvane & Thornhill. This picture shows Sprinter unit No 150001 arriving with the first service to use the new station.

Right:
Class 150 Sprinter No 150263 departs from Cardiff Queen Street on a Barry Island to Aberdare service on 27 April 1990. The recently installed through connection to the one time bay platform can be seen directly behind the second coach.
Kevin Lane

Below right:
Class 150 Sprinter No 150276 on a service from Rhymney to Penarth approaches Queen Street North Junction on 27 April 1990. This was the approximate site of the old Rhymney Parade station.
Kevin Lane

Right:
Railfreight Distribution
Class 47 No 47095
Southampton WRD Quality
Approved accelerates
through Cardiff on
27 September 1994 with
vans for the ISIS link depot
at Canton.

Author

Below:
Class 143 unit No 143602
on the shuttle service to and
from Queen Street stands at
Cardiff Bute Road on
6 September 1994. Today
only a single platform is in
use. The ex-Taff Vale
station building can be seen
directly behind the unit.
From the start of the winter
timetable Bute Road was
advertised as Cardiff Bay.

Author

between Cardiff and Aberdare and on 30 October 1992 between Cardiff and Maesteg. To supplement the services a number of new stations have been opened on both routes. Passenger services on all of the Valley lines have been revitalised with the introduction of new Sprinter trains which have also allowed the service frequencies to be increased, (the last of the conventional or 'heritage' DMUs were withdrawn from South Wales services on 10 May 1992). Currently there is a 20min interval service from Cardiff Central to Barry and Penarth, a 30min interval service to Coryton and Treherbert and a 1hr interval service to Merthyr, Aberdare and Maesteg. There are also a number of feeder bus services from outlying areas to the stations at Treherbert, Aberdare and Ystrad Rhondda. These are timed to connect with the train services and the conductors carry Portis ticket issuing machines and can therefore issue through tickets to any British Rail station.

The improvement in services has meant that during the last 10 years passenger numbers have shown a steady increase up to the current figure of about 10 million per annum.

The sectorisation of the various services meant that Platforms 1–4 at Cardiff Central were operated by InterCity. Valley services, which came under Regional Railways, use Platforms 6 and 7. Interestingly, there is no Platform 5, the platforms have not been renumbered since the removal of the old down bay in the 1960s. Today the station is operated by a staff of only 36 (at the turn of the century the station staff numbered 365). Cardiff Central is served by 108 up and 147 down passenger trains each weekday. During 1993 ticket barriers were once again installed on Platforms 6 and 7, resulting in an immediate upturn in revenue. During 1994 the remains of the old Riverside station (Platforms 8 and 9) were demolished and the site is now occupied by Semaphore House, a prefabricated office block which houses the various Railtrack managers. The rest of the site is now in use as a car park. The old Great Western goods offices, which at the time of writing are still intact, are shortly to be demolished and it has been suggested that the main station entrance could be moved to this area. Standing adjacent to Central station is the Cardiff Power Box. This box was opened on 27 March 1966 and controls the main line from Marshfield to **Llantrisant East, together with stretches of the Valley lines.**

Right:
The remains of Cardiff Riverside station pictured in October 1993, shortly before it was removed. Author

Below:
Another shot of Bute Road to show the Taff Vale Railway station building now in use as a railway museum.

Author

During 1988 Queen Street Station was modernised once again, the station entrance was refurbished and in September 1990 the Platform 3 line was altered to a through road for services to and from Bute Road (now Cardiff Bay). The station at Cardiff Bay is near the Industrial & Maritime Museum which is also situated in the docks area.

The final remains of the former Rhymney Railway station at Cardiff Parade, adjacent to Queen Street station, were demolished in 1989. The ex-Taff Vale Railway carriage and wagon works at Cathays (opened in 1846) and the large yard at Radyr were both closed during 1993. However at the time of writing the GWR engine shed at Radyr, although unused, is still standing.

The maintenance depot at Canton is now essentially divided into two parts. The main line diesel depot, built on the site of the old steam shed, is now operated by Transrail and has maintenance responsibility for 154 locomotives which apart from the South Wales fleet include 12 St Blazey Class 37s, 21 Class 60s and 27 Class 56s working from Wigan and Buxton. Depot facilities include a 50-ton lifting crane which is currently the only one in the country

continued on page 86

84

Right:
The station itself now comprises three through platforms. On the left is a Class 143 working the shuttle service from Queen Street to Bute Road, and at Platform 2, a Class 150 Sprinter departs for Cardiff Central with a service from Aberdare.

Author

Below right:
Class 56 No 56114 runs past Canton with an empty MGR service on 27 September 1994. The remains of the old steam depot water tank can be seen on the right together with Class 37 No 37906. The large building on the left is the old carriage shed currently in use by the ISIS group.

Author

Below:
The main entrance to Cardiff Central. Notice the fine pediment proclaiming the Great Western Railway, exposed during the refurbishment of the concourse in 1982. If current plans come to fruition, the main entrance will be switched to the south side of the station.

Author

Above:
A view of the east end of Cardiff Central taken from a window of the Central Hotel on 17 August 1993.
Author

Right
Class 60 No 60036 *Sgurr Na Ciche* passes through Cardiff Central on 27 September 1994 with an up trainload of steel coils.
Author

Below right:
The interior of the GWR carriage depot at Canton, now the main servicing shop for Regional Railways South Wales & West. Here on 6 September 1994 units 143601 and 158840 are undergoing maintenance. Notice how clean and tidy the depot is.
Author

(other than at the Brush Works) that is capable of lifting a Class 60 engine straight from the locomotive frame, and a Heganscheidt Ground wheel lathe. This latter machine is capable of reprofiling any wheelset either loose or *in situ*. In June 1992 the depot was awarded the ISO 9002 standard for excellence.

The old DMU depot,which is now operated as a separate concern by Regional Railways, has in recent years seen considerable investment and has been completely modernised in order to deal with new generation units. The refurbished depot now provides full servicing and heavy maintenance facilities for the South Wales & West Train Operating Unit and Cardiff Valley fleets. Within the main building a separate heavy maintenance shed has been erected to facilitate engine changes and other heavy underframe work. The depot is responsible for the maintenance of 11 Class 143s,18 Class 153s, 23 Class 150s and 39 Class 158s for the South Wales West TOU and 14 Class 143s and 18 Class 150s for Valley Line services. Until May 1994 the depot also provided overnight servicing for up to two InterCity IC125 sets but since then this work has been undertaken at Landore. In August 1994 a new traincrew depot was opened adjacent to Cardiff Central at Wood Street.

Above right:
This second shot shows the main shed building with examples of Classes 143,150 and 158 awaiting their next tour of duty.
Author

Below right:
A view of the main loco yard at the Transrail depot at Canton on 6 September 1994, with Class 47 No 47213 Marchwood Military Port, and Nos 37157, 37263, 37031, 37258, 56016 and 56114.
Author

Right:
The exterior of the main repair shop at Transrail Canton on 27 September 1994. Class 56 No 56059 stands outside.
                                                    Author

Below right:
The interior of the main repair shop on 27 September 1994. Undergoing repair are Class 56 No 56033 and Class 31 No 31420.
                                                    Author

Inter City Shuttle services between Swansea, Cardiff and London are operated using IC125 sets (introduced on these services in October 1976!). These give an hourly interval service to and from Paddington with an average journey time between Cardiff and Paddington of 125min. Cross Country services from Cardiff to Brighton, Portsmouth, Devon and Cornwall, West Wales, Birmingham, Nottingham and Manchester are operated by Regional Railways using mainly Class 158 units. These services have now been running for a number of years but two particularly interesting workings which started during 1994 operate from Cardiff through to Waterloo where they connect with the European Passenger Network. The first of these runs via Warminster and Basingstoke and is operated by Regional Railways using a Class 158 unit. The second service is operated by InterCity using an IC125 set and runs via Kensington Olympia. The long running service to and from the north east is now operated using IC125s and leaves Swansea at 07.15 and Newcastle at 13.38, both trains currently run via Bristol.

The improved availability of the Class 143 and 150/2 units now allows the extensive valley line service to be operated using 32 two-car sets.

The area still sees a considerable amount of freight traffic comprising oil, steel, aggregates, iron ore and coal. These are hauled by Classes 37, 47, 56 and, since 1991, Class 60

locomotives. The conveyance of coal has diminished in recent years with the closure of many collieries. Maerdy, the last mine in the Rhondda valley, closed on 30 June 1986, whilst in the Taff Vale, only one mine, Tower Colliery, survives. Coal traffic today mainly comprises services from Port Talbot docks (imported) to the steel works at Llanwern and to the power station at Aberthaw. Iron Ore is also shipped into Port Talbot for rail delivery to Llanwern. Merry-go-round coal services also run from Cwmbargoed to Aberthaw. To the east of Cardiff, Pengam Freightliner Terminal is served by services to and from Tees Yard but the site may also be used for Channel Tunnel traffic. Pengam is also the junction for the sole remaining dock line which runs down to the Cardiff Tidal Terminal Complex. Since April 1993 Tidal Yard, which at one time contained 100 sidings, has been operated by locomotives and staff of the Allied Steel & Wire Company. In recent years the yard has been reduced to eight sidings which now serve a Petroleum Depot and the Allied Steel & Wire works.

Future developments in the area may see Aberdare line passenger services extended to Hirwaun with a new intermediate station at Trecynon. Proposals have been made to extend the service from Cardiff to Barry along all or part of the freight-only Vale of Glamorgan route to give a Cardiff–Barry–Bridgend service. A slightly more contentious issue is the proposal to construct a new rail link into Cardiff Rhoose Airport from the Vale of Glamorgan line. Rejected at one stage by BR, under the new regime this may yet happen. Finally, the waterfront area at Cardiff is also undergoing change with the construction of new trading estates and other dockside developments such as a Maritime Museum, shops, a leisure centre and a marina.

Above:
Nos 37668, 08953 and 56001 stand outside the wheel lathe shop at Canton on 27 September 1994. The building was constructed in 1989 and houses a Heganscheidt ground wheel lathe.
Author

Below right:
Pride of Canton Depot is Class 56 No 56044 Cardiff Canton Quality Assured seen here passing through Cardiff Central on 27 September 1994 in newly applied Transrail livery.
Author

CHAPTER 8
Locomotive and
Carriage Works

The first locomotive works to be established in Cardiff was constructed by the Taff Vale Railway at West Yard. Built in around 1845, the West Yard works was situated between the company's Dock station at Bute Street and the Glamorganshire Canal. Access to the site, which was at right angles to the docks line, was a major problem and was made via a turntable situated at the north end of the Docks station from where locomotives had to be towed across Bute Street.

The West Yard factory, although cramped, was fully equipped to deal with all aspects of locomotive and boiler construction and until the turn of the century the company built many of its locomotives here. It must have been a busy place as, apart from locomotive construction, a considerable amount of repair and rebuilding work was also undertaken. The works were enlarged over the years to cope with the increasing locomotive fleet (in 1845 the company owned just 16 locomotives while by 1920 the total had risen to 275). After the Grouping much of the work was switched by the Great Western to the former Rhymney Railway Works at Caerphilly. The West Yard factory was closed on 31 August 1926, the last engine to be repaired, ex Taff Vale '02' class No 412, having left the works just a few days earlier on **28 August.**

Previous page:
Pilot loco No 796 moving ex-Taff Vale 'M1' class 0-6-2T No 481 (TV No 86) together with ex-Taff Vale 'U' class 0-6-2T No 602 (TV No 30) across the Bute Street crossing and into the West Yard works on 6 August 1926.

Right:
The main erecting shop at West Yard on 23 April 1926. In shot are Nos 917 an ex-Taff Vale 'K' class 0-6-0 (TV No 284), 43 an ex-Rhymney Railway Class R 0-6-2T (RR No 47) and 287 a Taff Vale Class 04 0-6-2T (TV No 47).

Below right:
West Yard works was opened by the Taff Vale Railway in 1845. Locomotives entered the works via a turntable near the docks station, and a level crossing over Bute Street. This picture shows the old machine shop at West Yard on 23 April 1926. The works was closed by the GWR on 1 August 1926.

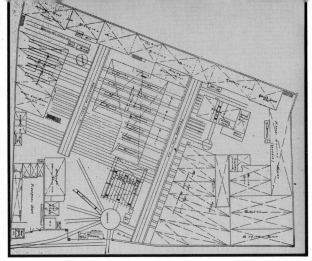

Above:
Plan of the West Yard locomotive works dating from around the turn of the century.

Above right:
0-6-2T No481 on the traversing table at West Yard on 6 August 1926. The traversing table was situated between the erecting and boiler shops.

Below right:
Ex-Taff Vale 0-6-0ST No 796 (Taff Vale No 265) on pilot duty stands on the turntable just north of Cardiff Docks station on 6 August 1926. The locomotive is being turned for entry into the West Yard repair shops.

The Taff Vale had also opened its own carriage and wagon works to the north of Cardiff at Cathays in 1846. Over the years the company both constructed and repaired all of its extensive carriage and wagon fleet here. Civil Engineering facilities were added in about 1892. After the Grouping the works were modernised by the Great Western, the company having previously concentrated all carriage construction at Swindon, and in 1929 several of the old repair shops were demolished and replaced by a new larger building. The new wagon repair shop was duly opened in August 1931. It was clearly the GWR's intention to concentrate all carriage and wagon repairs at Cathays and in July 1932 the Carriage & Wagon Department at Caerphilly was closed with all work being transferred to Cathays. The works saw little change in the ensuing years and by the 1980s work at Cathays comprised the conversion and repair of wagons and coaching stock and also the maintenance of Civil Engineers' track machines, Cathays being the main South Wales centre of the Civil Engineers department. Sadly the recession of the last few years caused a general downturn of business and the carriage and wagon repair shops at Cathays were finally closed on 19 March 1993. *continued on page 94*

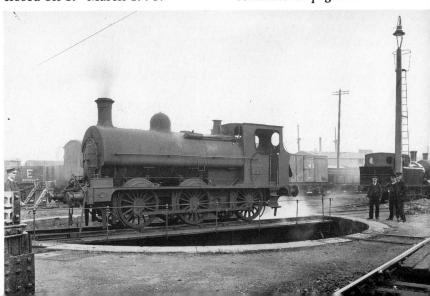

Above right:
The last engine to leave West Yard works was No 412, a TVR '02' class (No 31). It is pictured here on 28 August 1926 surrounded by some of the works staff.

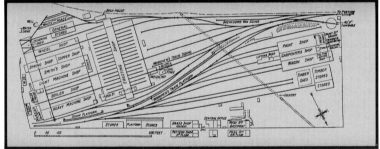

Right:
A general view of the ex-Rhymney Railway locomotive works at Caerphilly. The new erecting shop constructed by the GWR in 1925/6 can be seen on the right.

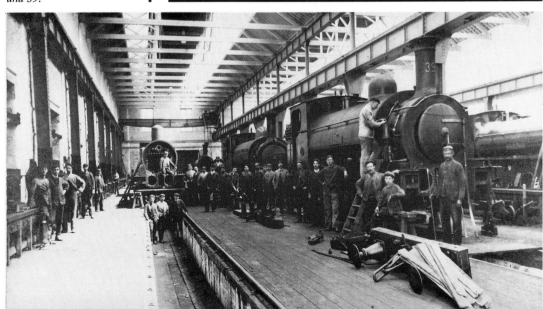

Below right:
Plan of the locomotive works at Caerphilly as rebuilt by the Great Western in 1926.

Bottom:
The interior of the original erecting shop at Caerphilly taken in July 1906. Locos in view are Taff Vale 0-6-2STs Nos 39, 81 and 59.

Above:
A view of the new erecting shop at Caerphilly pictured shortly after completion in 1926.

Right:
This general view of the yard at Caerphilly was taken on the occasion of a Gloucester Railway Society trip on 12 June 1956. The special train hauled by an ex-Taff Vale 'A' class 0-6-2T No 391 and 'Dean Goods' 0-6-0 No 2538 can be seen alongside the works halt.

W. Potter

Below right:
The carriage shop at Caerphilly pictured here on 2 May 1962 and just two days before closure.

The Rhymney Railway Company had established a small works at its Cardiff Bute Docks terminus in October 1857. Initially, there were two main buildings, a locomotive shop and a carriage shop; these were situated adjacent to the company's locomotive depot. The RR did not construct its own locomotives so the works were used for repairs only. By the 1890s, and with an increasing locomotive fleet, the company was looking to expand the docks works but being unable to purchase the land required it decided to construct a new works. The site, which measured 17 acres in area, was situated only seven miles north of Cardiff at Wernddu, and adjacent to the small town of Caerphilly. Completion of the new works in December 1901 saw the old docks works closed; the redundant buildings being incorporated into the adjacent locomotive depot. Carriage repairs were also switched from here to the company's existing workshops at Cathays. The remains of the old Docks works were swept away in 1930 to allow for the construction of Cardiff East Dock shed.

The Rhymney Railway locomotive workshops at Caerphilly were by far the largest in Wales, and although finished in February 1901 were not finally opened until December of the same year, due apparently to difficulties in the installation of **heavy plant.**

Below right:
The interior of the main erecting shop taken on Wednesday 27 March 1963 and showing the last four engines to be repaired at Caerphilly. From left to right: '5600' class No 6672, 'Grange' class No 6813 Eastbury Grange, '7200' class No 7228 and the very last engine to leave the works (on 16 April 1963) '5200' class No 5203.
E. Mountford

Below:
The end of the line for 0-6-0PT No 8468 as it is cut up at Caerphilly on 23 May 1960.
E. Mountford

Above:
Another picture taken on the same day shows the main carriage repair shop at Cathays.

Above right:
The paint shop at the Taff Vale carriage and wagon shops at Cardiff Cathays pictured on 22 April 1926.

Below:
Cardiff Cathays looking north on 8 October 1931. On the left is Cathays yard and on the right the carriage and wagon works.
British Rail

The Grouping saw the Great Western locomotive fleet in South Wales increase by almost 800. Many of the pre-Grouping companies had their own small repair works dotted around the South Wales system which was not a very efficient arrangement for the newly enlarged GWR. At this time the main workshops at Swindon were working to their limit, so the company decided to close all of these small repair shops and concentrate repairs for all South Wales locomotives (other than express types) at Caerphilly. To do this the old Rhymney works were modernised and enlarged with the construction of a new three-bay erecting shop, served by overhead cranes and a central traverser. The new works, which had a capacity of 60 locomotives, was opened in August 1926. The carriage works was also modernised by the Great Western during 1939 with the construction of a new paint shop and lifting shop, both being opened on 28 August 1939.

Generally the locomotive works was used for the repair of tank engines but in later years Caerphilly undertook work on all types of Great Western locomotives (with the exception of 'Kings'). The 1960s brought a rundown of work at Caerphilly and on 4 May 1962 the carriage works closed. The rapid run down of steam traction also saw locomotive repairs decline and the works finally closed on 29 June 1963. After closure the site was designated the 'Harold Wilson Industrial Estate' and today 32 years after closure many of the buildings are still *in situ* and in industrial use. For many years a special works train was operated to take staff to and from the works, initially running from Caerphilly station into the small

works platform but in later years the service ran to and from Cardiff Queen Street. The last works train hauled by 060PT No 9480 departed from the small works platform on Friday 28 June 1963.

Yet another locomotive works was situated eight miles south of Cardiff at Barry. The Barry Railway had opened its own small locomotive works in 1893. The works were situated adjacent to the locomotive depot and was responsible for the maintenance of the company's 148 locomotives as well as much of its rolling stock. The works buildings comprised a main erecting shop, a boiler shop, a foundry and a carriage repair shop. Interestingly, after the Grouping the works was retained and continued in use for light locomotive and carriage repairs. In December 1957 the carriage repair shop at Barry was placed under the control of the Caerphilly works manager. The run down of steam traction saw the last steam locomotive to be repaired leave the works on 24 December 1959, thereafter the building was used for wagon repairs until it was finally closed during 1964.

Above:
An undated picture but possibly taken in the 1920s shows a group of staff at Cathays carriage and wagon works.

Below right:
A sad shot of the last locomotive to be repaired at Barry, '5600' class 0-6-2T No 5684, seen here inside the works on the final day of operation, 24 December 1959.

Bottom right:
The interior of the erecting shop at Barry on 8 May 1959 with from left to right '5600' class 0-6-2Ts Nos 5641, 6644 and 5687.
                          E. Mountford

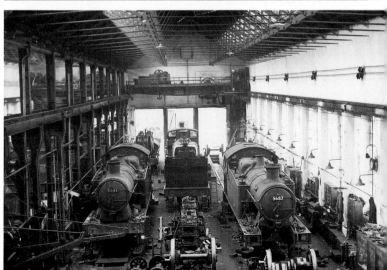